The Pocket Muse
Endless Inspiration

The Pocket Muse
Endless Inspiration

NEW
IDEAS FOR
WRITING

Monica Wood

WRITER'S DIGEST BOOKS
Cincinnati, Ohio
www.writersdigest.com

The Pocket Muse: Endless Inspiration © 2006 by Monica Wood. Manufactured in China. All rights reserved. No part of this book may be reproduced in any form or by any electronic or mechanical means including information storage and retrieval systems without permission in writing from the publisher, except by a reviewer, who may quote brief passages in a review. Published by Writer's Digest Books, an imprint of F+W Publications, Inc., 4700 East Galbraith Road, Cincinnati, OH 45236. (800) 289-0963. First edition.

Distributed in Canada by Fraser Direct, 100 Armstrong Avenue, Georgetown, ON, Canada L7G 5S4, Tel: (905) 877-4411. Distributed in the U.K. and Europe by David & Charles, Brunel House, Newton Abbot, Devon, TQ12 4PU, England, Tel: (+44) 1626 323200, Fax: (+44) 1626 323319, E-mail: postmaster@davidandcharles.co.uk. Distributed in Australia by Capricorn Link, P.O. Box 704, Windsor, NSW 2756 Australia, Tel: (02) 4577-3555.

Visit our Web site at www.writersdigest.com for information on more resources for writers. To receive a free weekly e-mail newsletter delivering tips and updates about writing and about Writer's Digest products, register directly at our Web site at http://newsletters.fwpublications.com.

10 09 08 07 06   5 4 3 2 1

Library of Congress Cataloging-in-Publication Data
Wood, Monica.
  The pocket muse : endless inspiration : new ideas for writing / by Monica Wood. – 1st ed.
     p. cm.
  ISBN-13: 978-1-58297-419-4 (alk. paper)
  ISBN-10: 1-58297-419-5 (alk. paper)
  1. Authorship. I. Title.   2006022272
  PN147.W575 2006
  808'.02--dc22

Edited by Jane Friedman
Designed by Grace Ring, based on a design by Lisa Kuhn
Production coordinated by Robin Richie and Mark Griffin

Photographs on pages 11, 49, 52, 69, 88, 104, 115, 124, 142, 157, 165, 187, 204, 208, and 211 by Grace Ring.

Photographs on pages 9, 22, 25, 38, 43, 48, 66, 84, 87, 91, 92-93, 99, 109, 112, 113, 132, 138, 143, 145, 147, 158, 161, 168-69, 182, 193, and 212 by Bob Thompson.

Photograph on page 148 from the family archive of Monica Wood.

For Patrick Clary

and for my teachers: Burt deFrees, Anne

Wood, and Roland Flint (*in memoriam*)

Acknowledgments

For this second volume of *The Pocket Muse*,
the author owes many thanks to Grace Ring,
for her gorgeous design; to Jane Friedman,
for rowing the boat to shore; and to Bob
Thompson, for another batch of photographs
that engage the imagination.

About the Author

Monica Wood is the author of three novels, *Any Bitter Thing*, *My Only Story*, and *Secret Language*, and a book of connected stories, *Ernie's Ark*. Her stories have been widely anthologized, selected for the Pushcart Prize, and read on public radio, most recently on NPR's "Selected Shorts." Her previous titles for Writer's Digest Books include *The Pocket Muse* and *Description* (Elements of Fiction series).

Introduction

I wrote the final draft of this book in October 2005, largely in the Bibliothèque St. Jean-Baptiste in Quebec City, Canada, a six-hour drive north from my home in Portland, Maine. In the neighborhood where my husband and I sublet a chilly, weather-worn apartment with a single floor lamp and a half-broken fridge, we were the only Anglophones. Dan and I woke every day to the sound of schoolchildren squabbling in French on their way to school, and went to sleep every night to the metronomic beat of French hip-hop funneling down our narrow street from one of the other whitewashed brick buildings with gaily painted doors. Even though my home kitchen—with its double-insulated windows and working appliances—was but a half day's drive away; even though I spoke serviceable French and could get most of what I needed on the first try; even though the province of Quebec was the friend and neighbor with whom we Mainers shared a geographical border, several TV stations, and generations' worth of family connections, I felt a foreigner's discombobulation for a solid week, a homesickness so profound it felt like a literal weight in my body.

Dan, who speaks about thirty words of French, no more than three of which can logically appear in the same sentence, is a far more equable soul than I. He did what he always does when faced with discombobulation: he went to work. On our first evening in the city of wine and chocolate, he relieved the tiny apartment freezer of four inches of packed ice, then fixed its broken door with, I'm not kidding, the clicker-thing from a ballpoint pen and a U-shaped spacer cut out of his mousepad. Then he filled the freshly denuded freezer with ice cream. He found a hardware store and installed brighter bulbs in the kitchen and a three-way for the lamp so that two people could read a book at the same time. Meanwhile, I was fretting about how cold we might get by month's end (you could stick your pinky through the window gaps) and wondering aloud whether the cat, a portly gent with double paws, was drinking too much water, a sure sign that we'd agreed to care for a diabetic short-timer who would die on our watch. I feared that our neighbors would not understand my French, and that I would not understand theirs. (On our second day, Dan bought some baking chocolate and informed the chocolatier in French that he planned to drive a cake.) And the car—oh, horrors, the car!—what were we to do about the car, for which we'd arranged no parking sticker, not anticipating the baffling Québecois interdictions on overnight parking, rush-hour parking, weekend parking, and parking on high holy days and full-moon Tuesdays?

You know the end of this story. The cat did not die. We did not freeze to death. The Francophones did not spit in our faces for puréeing verb tenses beyond recognition. In fact, the cat adored us, and lost a little weight. And after a handful of cold-nose days, we enjoyed one of the loveliest Indian summers in the history of weather. Our neighbors proved unfailingly decent and helpful and warm-hearted. Even the parking garage turned up a sunny atten-dant who, with the patience of a kindergarten teacher, walked us through the hokey-pokey of securing a monthly pass from a malevolent machine. In the drafty kitchen we toasted our good fortune with a hefty red wine from the local wine shop. We walked everywhere, worked well and hard on our respective projects, and when it came time to go home, I was the one who wanted most to stay.

This introduction is not, of course, about how lucky I was to have married Mr. Fixit. Or even about how stupid I was to spend seven precious days of my one and only life in Henny Penny mode, jumpy and fretful and unyielding when faced with the uncertain and unfamiliar. This story, like most stories, exists as metaphor: what is writing if not the great land of the unknown? The foreign tongue we'll never master? The teetery, trembling foray into a realm that might hurt us in private, or humiliate us in public, or, worse, uncover our thudding limitations?

The first *Pocket Muse* came to me as I was finishing a book of linked stories, the only easily won fiction I'd ever written; I don't remember ever being happier as a writer. The second *Pocket Muse* arrived on grimmer terms, as I faced mortal combat with a novel in progress, feeling stranded and miserable with my sheaf of false starts and dead ends. How, I wondered, after writing so many books—proof, surely, that I knew my way in, and out—could I once again be facing the familiar void, the same old blank page? Wasn't

this supposed to get easier? But there I was, back at the gate, hoping that the thing for which I had no name, no form, and no hope would nevertheless become, sooner or later, a story that held.

And so, unsurprisingly, *The Pocket Muse: Endless Inspiration* addresses the subject of artistic despair far more often than its predecessor. There's more here about what it means to attempt a creative life when everything around us pulls in the opposite direction. Also more than my usual trickle of self-revelation—I who so rarely venture into nonfiction and approach other people's memoirs with a touch of dread. In the end, I left the pages that bleed, because I wrote this book as much for myself, dear reader, as for you. The advice on technique, the writing prompts and exercises, the provocative photographs, the tales of the absurd, the quotations from other writers, the moral support and marching orders—they're for both of us. The advice on managing your time, your work, and your emotions—I'm speaking to myself as well as to you. You can open this book at random and, I hope, find comfort; or, absent that, good counsel; or, absent that, a shove out the door, or in the door, whichever applies.

Which is to say that I hope this book will do for you what it did for me. I composed this book as I failed to compose my novel in progress; I organized this book as I lost, utterly, my new novel's shape; I finished this book as I gave up on my novel in despair, ditching all those hard-won pages and starting over again. Writing this book of advice and inspiration kept me looking forward, not back, as I tried to reconnect with a novel that is still such a long way (years, I mean) from finding itself.

But I trust it will. I trust that sooner or later I'll reread this introduction and think, If only I'd known then what I know now. But of course I did know. Don't we always know? We keep writing until we find the story. Which brings me back to my sojourn in Quebec, and the time I wasted before finally giving in to the experience. The turning point

came when I found a library, the aforementioned Bibliothèque St. Jean-Baptiste, which for two centuries lived as a church and still looked almost exactly like the gilt-and-alabaster thing it always was. It smelled like church and sounded like church, and I surely did not overlook the significance of all those books residing in a consecrated place. It is faith, finally, that saves us: faith that our words will matter enough—if only to ourselves alone—to risk humiliation, or rejection, or failure.

This is no small thing we do.

Welcome to the journey.

"*How we spend our days
is, of course, how we
spend our lives.*"

—Annie Dillard,
from *The Writing Life*

{ How will you spend this day? }

Open an imaginary door.
What do you see?

Write about something on the verge
of collapse: *building, bridge,
marriage, contest, institution,
alliance, certainty*

Notice From the Department
of Procrastination Prevention

The top-performing item in my store of procrastination-
prevention equipment is the humble egg timer. I use a
cheap wind-up model—you can literally hear it through
my studio door—but after a minute or so I fail to notice
the ticking. Set the timer for anywhere from the minimum
to the maximum, open your laptop or writing pad, and
play a game of Beat the Clock. Whether you set a modest
goal of one sentence or an ambitious goal of one thousand words, chances are you'll have *something* underway
by the time the dinger goes off.

A Tip on Dialogue

Avoid letting characters repeat through dialogue what the reader already knows. For example, if Character A fights with Character B on page 12, don't let Character A recap the fight to Character C on page 20. Instead, *imply* the recap with something like:

> When Al told Charlie about his melodramatic fistfight with Bruno, Charlie looked unsurprised. "Big deal," he said. "Bruno fights with everybody."

Let the scene continue from there without a hitch. Every line of dialogue should feel like news.

"At our writing lab, 826 Valencia, we're trying to raise all these kids to believe that they are writers—and indeed they are—and convince them that they can go around and say, 'I am a writer,' or 'I am a poet,' at age twelve, and hopefully they will carry that conviction with them the rest of their lives."

—Vendela Vida, author of *And Now You Can Go*,
interviewed by Robert Birnbaum at identitytheory.com

I am a writer.

Ah, those four little words. Before I ever got published, I had a set of criteria: two short stories published or one thousand dollars earned from writing, and I'll be able to say them. Then, two short stories later, I upped the ante to four stories or four thousand dollars. Not until my first novel came out did I manage to say them—and only then with a dozen caveats and stipulations.

What the hell was I waiting for? I wrote every day for twelve years—*twelve years!*—before a single copy of my first novel appeared on a single bookstore shelf. Those four little words give me untold pleasure now, but I don't know whether it's because my feelings about myself have changed, or because the question "Have you published anything?" can now be answered in the unequivocal affirmative. Maybe it's *those* four words—

HAVE YOU PUBLISHED ANYTHING

—that give us pause, even though they have nothing to do with us and everything to do with the skeptic asking the question. Other people's definitions intimidated me. For all those years, I walked the walk but refused to proclaim myself.

{ In other words: Money, schmoney.
If you write, you're a writer. }

Write about the
inexplicable menace
in a seemingly
neutral object.

Tapping your fingers instead of the keys?
Try adding a song lyric to a sagging passage
and move on from there. Some possibilities
from the public domain:

"When you finally get back up on your feet again,
everybody wants to be your long lost friend."
— *"Nobody Knows You When You're*
Down and Out" by Jimmy Cox

"I didn't raise my boy to be a soldier,
I brought him up to be my pride and joy."
— *"I Didn't Raise My Boy to Be a Soldier"*
by Alfred Bryan and Al Piantadosi

"My head got wet with the midnight sky."
— *"Don't Be Weary, Traveler" (anon.)*

"There's no truth in our dreams."
— *"Where Are the Happy Dreams*
of Childhood?" (trad. Germany)

"Why, I wonder, is no letter coming?"
— *(trad. Bulgaria)*

"Oh there's no use talkin', folks, the panic's on."
— *"The Broadway Blues" by J. Brandon Walsh and Terry Sherman*

Five Questions to Ask During Revision

❶ What interests you most in this draft (poem, memoir, story, novel, essay, biography)? Why is this so interesting?

❷ Is the main character sympathetic? If not, are the character's motives and actions at least recognizable, understandable, plausible?

❸ Do we have enough information about the character and his/her circumstances, or does the draft seem to be hiding the heart of the matter?

❹ Conversely, do we have too much *information* and not enough *implication*?

❺ Do you believe in this world you've created?

Write about the one
who refuses to fit in.

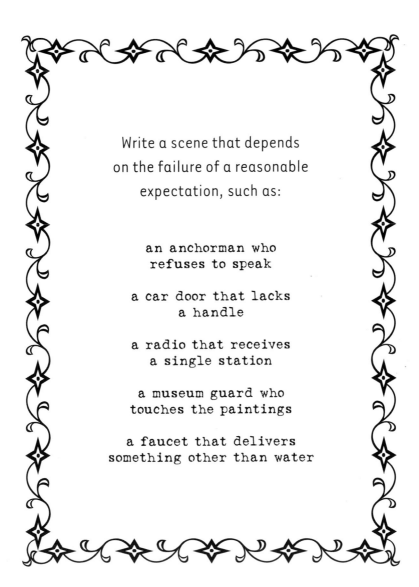

Write a scene that depends
on the failure of a reasonable
expectation, such as:

an anchorman who
refuses to speak

a car door that lacks
a handle

a radio that receives
a single station

a museum guard who
touches the paintings

a faucet that delivers
something other than water

A Wordsmith's Warmup

The catch-all term is *homonym*, but homonyms, technically defined, refer only to words that look and sound alike but differ in meaning. (For example, a gentleman in the stern might *bow* to the lady in the *bow*.) *Homophones* sound alike but differ in spelling and meaning (*straight* line, *strait* of Magellan). *Homographs* look alike but differ in sound and meaning (*bass* drum, *bass* fishing). No matter what you call them, mix up a batch of these entertaining words into a single paragraph and see what happens.

peak, peek, pique
rapt, wrapped, rapped
air, heir, err
dove (bird), dove (into the water)
foot (body), foot (measurement), foot (of bed, cliff), foot (the bill)
bough, bow (bend), bow (of boat), bow (in hair), Bo (name)
rein, rain, reign
clothes, close (shut), close (near)
serious, Sirius
wind (breeze), wind (turn), whined, wined
moderate (medium), moderate (to direct)
spring (season), spring (pounce), spring (coil)
column (of type), column (architecture)
sew, so, sow
ram (animal), ram (push)
you, yew, ewe
flew, flu, flue
raise, rays, raze
wait, weight

Write about the last
piece of something—pie,
real estate, posterity—

and the two people
who want it.

Write about a
household item
that becomes
the source of a
family war.

A man walks into a bar. But it isn't a bar.

A Tip on Style

Do refrain from dangling your modifiers in public. The dangling (or misplaced) modifier varies in type, but for our purposes let's call it a clause or phrase that appears to modify something it can't logically modify—with bizarre results.

Examples:

Sidetracked by the phone call, the stew boiled over and Ella blamed her chatty mother.

Was the stew sidetracked by the phone call? Try, "Sidetracked by the phone call, Ella let the stew boil over and blamed her chatty mother."

While drinking and laughing on the patio, several firetrucks distracted the happy revelers.

Surely the firetrucks aren't drinking and laughing. Try, "While drinking and laughing on the patio, the revelers were distracted by several firetrucks."

You can get into modifier trouble anywhere in a sentence, not just at the beginning. Examples:

Mary admired the dress I bought for her in a department store with puffed sleeves.

If you move the modifier close to the thing being modified, you're out of trouble: "Mary admired the dress with puffed sleeves, which I bought for her in a department store." Or: "Mary admired the puffed-sleeve dress that I bought for her in a department store."

I watched my uncle Max kill a two-pound snake as a little girl.

Again, the trick is to place the modifier as close as possible to the thing being modified: "As a little girl, I watched my uncle Max kill a two-pound snake."

Modifier-dangling is a dismayingly easy crime to commit. I'm a reliable offender myself, saved from public shame only through the good graces of my English-teacher sister.

My friend Beth, who teaches art to high school kids, encourages her students to search for the "found aesthetic" in their everyday lives. Here's the drill: Wherever you are—waiting for an oil change in the waiting room at Prompto; sitting on your stoop watching garbage roll down the street; lollygagging by a mountain stream listening to fish a-jumpin'—find an image that pleases you aesthetically. It might be the way a shadow meets a wall, or the shape of a stethoscope against a pillowy chest, or the movement of fringe on the sleeve of a jacket.

This exercise changed my life. Really. I believe it is no longer possible for me to waste time. Looking around right now, I catch several found aesthetics: a bright orange sidelight on an otherwise muddy truck, light flashing off the spirals of a notebook, shards of amber in my cat's green eyes, two large trees whose branches join high over the street as entwined fingers.

At the very least, this practice can increase your powers of observation and empathy, two essential writing tools.

"The book is a perfect form, a physical thing that you can carry with you, that survives power outages and doesn't need batteries. It's simple, it's aesthetically pleasing, and you can use it again and again."

—Annie Proulx,
author of *The Shipping News*

Remember the first book that ever thrilled you? How it smelled, what it weighed in your hand, how you felt as you opened the cover? Recall that exquisite feeling--part fulfillment, part desire--and write about it.

23

Memo From the Department
of Just Showing Up

Back in the late eighties, when I was sending out short stories and getting rejections back by the busload (top one-day total: six), I received a handwritten rejection from an editor at *Story* magazine. He liked my story, but the editor-in-chief rejected it. I sent him another—ditto. Seven years and many rejections later, that same editor wound up managing a book series on fiction-writing technique. He remembered my stories, had read my first novel, and thought I'd be a good bet to write one of the books in the series.

No stories of mine ever did see print in *Story* magazine. But because I kept submitting them in the hope that they would, I wound up publishing two books with that same editor.

If you keep your hat in the ring, sooner or later somebody's going to need a hat.

What's the most you ever paid
for something you didn't want?

{ Why did you fork over the dough? }

26

Some writers I know

play Solitaire or Minesweeper on their computer as a kind of palate cleanser between courses of writing. I prefer to get away from the screen and do something that allows me to move, if only minimally, while firing up a different set of synapses. My favorite: the Victorian puzzle, a set of nine tiles with diabolically similar images on each tile. The object is to match the tiles so that all nine images join up correctly, which is about four million times harder than you think.

These puzzles were the nineteenth-century version of the Rubik's Cube, and you can buy them today in museum stores or on eBay. I keep a small collection that I treasure for its beauty and whimsy. The particular concentration these puzzles require—attention, not thought—magically clears extra space for the thing I'm really working on.

Today-Only Writer's Special

Give another writer, someone more accomplished than you, a sincere and specific compliment.

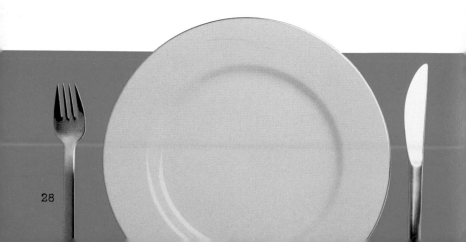

Five More Questions to Ask During Revision

❶ Is your language carefully crafted, or are there areas where the words lose precision?

❷ Does the dialogue illuminate character and advance the story?

❸ Is point of view consistent?

❹ Is point of view well chosen?

❺ If you've come up with a clever or un-usual gimmick (e.g., a surprise narrator, a reverse chronology), does the piece subsist on its own, beyond the gimmick?

Tips on Using the Tape Recorder as a Writing Tool

❶ Record someone talking about his or her job. Characters need jobs, and there is no substitute for the horse's mouth.

❷ If you can stand it, record yourself reading your own work, then play it back, listening for shoddy constructions, feeble dialogue, flabby transitions, and other hair-raising crimes against the English language.

❸ Record people whose diction you find appealing or unusual. If they don't know what to say, ask them to tell you how they got their first apartment, or about their first day of school.

❹ You can also record nonhuman voices—animals, rain, machinery—in the event you'll need an accurate reference for a future description.

A Tip on Tension

Writing suspenseful passages can be a tricky business. Interestingly, a headlong, multi-part sentence can heighten suspense just as effectively as a string of short, staccato ones. Which style you choose depends on whether you want the reader's heart to go pitty-pat (short, staccato) or her stomach to do a long rollercoaster flip (headlong, multi-part). The key is to maintain a rhythm. Compare:

Rollercoaster: Effraim hummed nervously under his breath, a habit he'd affected as a child whenever he felt threatened, though it did no good now as he crept up the long, curved stairway toward a blade of light that glowed beneath the door.

Pitty-pat: Effraim crept up the stairs. An empty hallway. A shut door. A blade of light. One more step. The light widened. Closer now. He began to hum, a childhood instinct that failed to calm him.

If you are reading this in springtime,

probably you've been overtaken by the great wash of changed air, the notion of bees waking in the hive, the blinding joy of longer sunshine and tiny grass shoots and the emerging cycle of life, blah, blah, blah. Beware, writer friends! This is the season when our worst sentimental impulses take over, and the Muse sits smoking in a corner, rolling her eyes. As trees twitter with returning birds, write some cold, dark, wintry prose. Possible kick-starts:

a man **skulking** under
a darkened Wal-Mart sign

four girls in a **freezing** courtroom

a car **skidding** over black ice

{ If you are reading this in winter, do the opposite: write some sprightly, spring-green prose. }

"Time is on my side."
—Mick Jagger

P.D. James published her first book, *Cover Her Face*, at age 42.

Rachel Carson published her first book, *Silent Spring*, at age 54.

Annie Proulx published her first book, *Postcards*, at age 58.

Penelope Fitzgerald published her first novel, *The Golden Child*, at age 61.

Frank McCourt published his first book, *Angela's Ashes*, at age 66.

Peter Pouncey published his first book, *Rules for Old Men Waiting*, at age 67.

Harriet Doerr published her first book, *Stones for Ibarra*, at age 73.

Helen Hooven Santmyer published her first bestseller, "*... And Ladies of the Club*," at age 88.

{ You have time to live an entire life as something else, and then become a writer. }

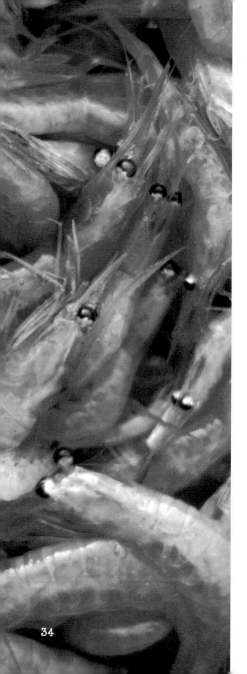

Revising a long piece—a novel, a biography, a memoir—poses such difficulty because you can't hang it on the wall, like a painting, and see the whole thing at once. Shorter forms can be laid across a table, page by page, but a book-length project lives largely in the mind even when you have a heap of pages to prove its existence. In your mind and in reality, the thing looks like a blob of goo, repulsive and potentially dangerous.

Just as you would divide up tasks in a room that needs cleaning, divide your piece into accomplishable parts. For example:

- a single scene
- page 20
- a part that belongs to Character A
- a part that belongs to Character B
- the closing paragraph
- the transition on page 185
- the dialogue in Chapter 6
- the narrative in Chapter 7

A single task won't crush your spirit. Give yourself a break.

Recount the history of
a vehicle you once loved.

Memo From the Department
of True Confessions

Not long ago, insomniac and restless, I found myself at 12:30 on a Wednesday night slumped across my couch watching a rerun of *Ellen*. When Barry Manilow came on to chat about his new CD and sing that awful "her name was Lola" song for the studio audience, I experienced an apocalyptic epiphany, calculating instantly all the hours of my one and only life buried forever in the marrow-sucking badlands of television programming. I stood up, yanked the plug out of the wall, hoisted the beast into my arms, and shoved it into the guest room until I could figure out how to destroy it altogether. When I finally got to bed, my half-asleep husband asked, "Where've you been?" "Reading," I lied, and eventually fell asleep.

The next morning I resolved to make my lie come true. In the space left by the TV, I arranged a bowl of seashells, a stack of

hardcover books, a vase of irises. I hung a painting I'd bought in Quebec City, a gorgeous depiction of a pouch filled with eighteenth-century love letters. How magnificent this felt! Yes, this was the true reflection of my inner life! I love Art ! I love Books! I love Flowers! I hate TV!

On the following Tuesday, I rescued the television from exile in order to watch the final installment of *American Idol*. I had come to care whether Carrie Underwood or Bo Bice would win the big recording contract.

Reader, imagine my shame.

Fortunately, my epiphany and subsequent slipup coincided with my city's Heavy Item Pickup week, so I kicked the thing to the curb. Smokers do this all the time, I suppose, but it costs a lot more than three bucks to buy another pack of TV shows.

I could say: Hey, at least I didn't have cable! I watched

nighttime shows only! My TV was an early nineties relic that didn't cover an entire wall! None of these pathetic rationalizations dresses up the naked fact that I was not in complete control of my viewing habits. I watched TV out of boredom, or to avoid the blues, or to turn off my brain after a busy day. I share this ignominy in case you, who are reading this in recognition rather than disgust, may wish to know what happened after I kicked the habit.

I started writing a little bit at night, a pleasure I hadn't known since college, but otherwise not much changed outwardly. Instead of watching TV shows several evenings a week (full disclosure: *Everybody Loves Raymond* on Mondays; *American Idol* on Tuesdays; *The West Wing* on Wednesdays; and *CSI* on Thursdays), I added a few hours a week to my reading time, dispatched a few overdue household chores, and returned phone calls more promptly.

But something did change inwardly. Getting rid of the TV meant getting rid of one more source of meaningless noise. The inside of my head felt different. Less like a sidewalk garage sale and more like a treeless plain. Even my dreams felt less trammeled. Calm moved in where once reigned chaos. Days felt longer and more fillable.

It is possible that by the time you read this I will once again own a TV. I may decide that a writer cannot afford to be completely disconnected from the central conduit of popular culture. I may decide I can't do without televised basketball games. If so, I plan to arm myself with the memory of my midnight epiphany and do battle with my slothful impulses. Any bets?

"*[Fiction] is the only art form that makes us understand that other people's interior lives are as rich and complicated as our own, and I think anything that increases our empathy for other human beings and lets us see the world freshly in all its complexity is a useful thing.*

– Andrea Barrett, author of *Ship Fever* and *Servants of the Map*, speaking on *The News Hour*.

Empathy is every writer's stock in trade—not just the fiction writer's—because to empathize we must first observe. Think of the last time you got the feeling somebody was angry, or blue, or hiding something, despite his assurances to the contrary. How did you know the truth? A finger twitch? A barely perceptible change in eye color? A certain cant of the shoulders? A quiver in voice timbre? How, exactly, do we come to know the things we know?

Practice articulating the minute ways in which you suddenly understand another person's inner weather. These articulations make the world you write about recognizable to your readers, who will detect in your words something of themselves—and something of everybody they know.

Change a "no" to
a "yes" and watch
what happens.

FAQ #1

Do I need an agent?

Maybe. But does an agent need you? If you're selling magazine articles, poems, individual short stories, single essays—in short, anything that's not a book and won't bring in much money—an agent has scant incentive to take you on. Besides, you can probably sell your magazine and journal pieces just as well, or badly, as an agent can. If you have a book of poetry, your most reasonable outlet is a university press, and most of them acquire poetry manuscripts through award contests.

However, if you're peddling book-length prose—a memoir of your year with the rodeo, an analysis of the Hoover administration, essays on the birds of Borneo, a novel or story collection—then you need an agent whether she needs you or not.

Don't try to sell a book alone. Your heart will be left on the road like a squashed frog.

Write about somebody else's
mortification.

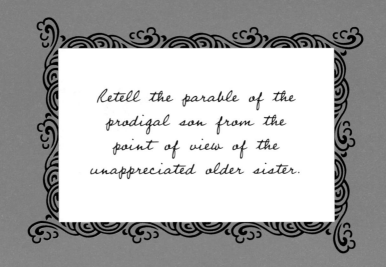

Retell the parable of the prodigal son from the point of view of the unappreciated older sister.

A Tip on Style

When describing an inanimate object, try to include a single animating element: a bird's shadow whisking across the side of a building, an anticipatory crackle from a bag of gumdrops, a fingerprint dried into a freshly painted mailbox. These details suggest a presence beyond the object and may lead you to a more nuanced understanding of the thing you are trying to describe.

44

Write about a
friendship that
failed you.

Write about a
friendship that
you failed.

Insert one of the following
into a moribund scene for
an instant wake-up:

an aggressive panhandler
four sealed boxes
poison ivy
a stranger at the door
mice

Write about confinement: physical or mental,
welcome or unwelcome, imaginary or real.

Write about a man seeking safety
from a woman who is not safe.

*Write about the
one who can't
resist applause.*

Write about the one who got away— and regretted it.

Five More Questions to Ask During Revision

❶ Do factual inaccuracies rob the draft of authority?

❷ Similarly, does incorrect punctuation, spelling, or usage rob the draft of authority?

❸ Does the piece bog down with unnecessary "business," such as introductions, or hellos and goodbyes?

❹ Does this draft seem the right length for its breadth and depth?

❺ Are you ready to identify that one nettlesome worry that has troubled you just under the surface while writing this draft?

Today-Only Writer's Special

Imagine just one reader, someone who will receive your words with enthusiasm and good will. Write for that one reader today.

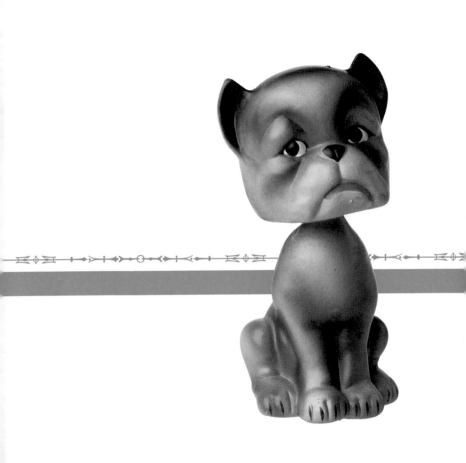

Identify your most unloved possession. How did you acquire this thing? Why did you think you needed it? How did it disappoint you?

L.A Weekly:
When you were away from fiction for all those many years, didn't you yearn for it?

Marilynne Robinson:
I am always engrossed in whatever I am doing. If a novel, a voice and a circumstance had not engaged my attention, I would have been absorbed by nonfiction and by teaching. I am glad to have written *Gilead*. It was an interesting experience, very important to me. But that intervening time was also good and important.

I love this answer by Marilynne Robinson, author of *Housekeeping* and *Gilead*. People frequently ask me how I write, when I write, what kind of pen I use, or where and when I get my ideas. Rarely am I asked what I do in my nonwriting hours. I make my bed, boil eggs, entertain children, read, dig holes, sing, sit around, edit manuscripts, watch birds, laugh or cry with my friends, lift weights, visit my family, hang out with my husband, wait in airport lines, buy groceries, count change ... I am just as alive and engaged when I am not writing as when I am.

Robinson took her sweet old time bringing out her second novel and appears to have no regrets. Quite the contrary, in fact.

{ Do you cherish your fallow times as much as you cherish your productive times? }

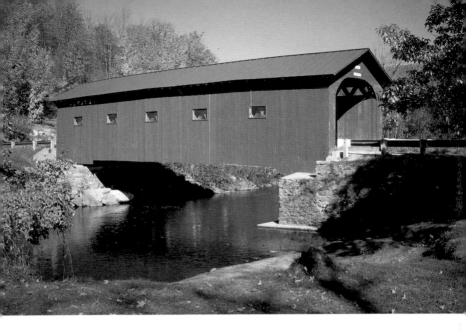

A Tip on Revision

At some point during an early to middle draft, set the work aside and spend a few hours asking yourself leading questions. Examples:

> Why is Rasheed so angry with Martina?
> How did Percy get this job in the first place?
> What's the worst thing that could happen to Leticia now that she's been discharged?
> What would happen if Frank refused the award?
> Who lived in Annabelle's apartment before she did?

Revision is not supposed to get you from point A to point B in record time. Revision is supposed to stroll you down all those roads not taken. And sometimes it burns all the bridges on those charming roads, leaving you no way back but the hard way back.

Memo From the Department of Slow Time

Letter writing composes my soul like nothing else. Not e-mail; I mean the kind of letters you put inside an envelope and hand over to the nice man at the post office, entrusting him with a little bitty piece of your heart. Letter writing serves as an antidote to the pace and clamor of contemporary life.

One of my dearest possessions at the moment is a sealing-wax kit. You know the kind: you light the little candle (excuse me, the taper) and let it drip onto the back of your envelope, then you press the blob of wax with a metal seal that bears your initial, or the face of a cat, or an unfurling flower. There is something about ritualizing writing (most writers do, in one form or another) that helps us treasure it.

Of course, first you have to write the letter. I'm down to the tiniest handful of friends with whom I correspond this way, and none of those can compare to my oldest correspondence, now going on thirty years old, with my friend Patrick Clary, a palliative care physician who is far too busy to write letters and yet finds time to write me at least once a month without fail. He is also—no surprise here—a poet. When he moved from New

York to New Hampshire, a mere 52 miles from my front doorstep, our correspondence took no notice of the convenience. The fact is, Patrick and I communicate differently in writing than in person, and neither of us is inclined to exchange one method for the other. In our letters over the years we have explored the themes that inform our writing: grief, loss, politics, family, literature, work, friendship. Life and death, in other words. Some letters are clearly first drafts, a stab at articulating something that will later—sometimes many years later—show up in one of his poems or one of my stories. This correspondence is a touchstone of my writing life.

It is never too late to begin such a correspondence, and the rewards are rich and legion.

{ Whom shall you choose? }

Here's an entertaining jump-start for a class or writing group. Ask everybody to start writing something, anything, in which the first sentence contains the word "private." Then, every forty-five seconds, the exercise leader shouts out another word that must be used as instantly as possible. This one is especially useful for people who have trouble getting started.

Sample shout-outs (words with double meanings work best):

column	spring
tire	bail
ram	clogging
riveted	break

Follow-up Notice From the Department of Procrastination Prevention

Most screen-saver programs have a "marquee" option, which allows you to type something that scrolls endlessly across the screen. I set mine to appear after thirty seconds of inactivity. The current one reads, "Don't get up."

Other scrolling marquees I've used:

Remember why you do this.

This thing won't finish itself.

What are you waiting for?

Some tips for joining, forming, or breaking up with a writing group

Some writers swear by writing groups; others scorn them. My one experience with a writing group was limited (a group of only three that met for two years) but exquisite. I recall the work on my third book as unmitigated joy, and it strikes me now that the vision and good humor and sharp critiquing of Andy and Natalie is largely responsible.

We met in one of three places: my house in Portland; Natalie's house in Waterville; or Andy's house upcountry, which included two Rhodesian ridgebacks, one a soulful old lady named Tula, the other a sixty-pound puppy with no respect whatsoever for the punctuated silences of literary discourse. We were serious, devoted, focused, and definitely not for everybody. Some might have found us too technically oriented; others might have found us not structured enough. What matters is that this group, at this time, worked magic for everybody in it.

I'd be hard pressed to replicate this trio now, but I did learn something about what I require should I ever try. Your requirements may differ, and even change over time, depending on what you're working on. I know groups who have met religiously for years, even decades, utterly unchanged. Others ebb and flow and re-form. Given the range of writing groups, it is hard to imagine anything close to an all-purpose set of guidelines, but the following questions may help you determine what kind of group you're getting into and whether it will meet your needs. If you're thinking of starting a new group or refocusing an old one, these questions will help you fine-tune your group's identity.

❶ How often does the group meet?

❷ Is the venue conducive to discussion? (A library meeting room or an apartment with three toddlers?)

❸ Does one style, genre, or school of writing predominate, or are all writers welcome?

❹ Are the group members more or less equal in experience, with similar goals, or a mixed group with varying levels of commitment and ambition?

❺ Has the group established standards for continued membership, e.g., requirements for attendance or output?

❻ What is the ratio of social time to discussion time? Does the group divide the time neatly, or are the sessions more free-flowing?

❼ How are discussions led? Is there a designated leader? If so, does the leader change with each session?

❽ How long is each session, and how many works are discussed per session?

❾ Do the sessions ever include writing, or are they devoted exclusively to critique?

❿ Are the works mailed to group members in advance, or are critiques done on the spot?

⓫ Has a critique protocol been worked out regarding who speaks when, or how much, if any, input the author gets while the discussion is going on?

⓬ Is the purpose of the group to offer support and encouragement only? Some writing groups dispense altogether with critique.

If you're in a group that doesn't suit you, jump ship now. Working with even *one* person who can help you stay on task beats languishing in a group that doesn't share your writing goals. No need for elaborate apologies; just say that your work needs privacy right now, which will afford you a graceful and vaguely mysterious exit.

Whenever writing seems impossibly hard, be glad your passion didn't point you to something like professional ice skating. Imagine what your triple lutz would look like at this point. By contrast, your writing is surely *better* than it was when your kneecaps still had all their padding. Your sense of language, structure, pacing, story, and all the etceteras improve as you age. Recurring themes begin to reveal themselves; your true subject appears at last. Life's crushing losses and inimitable triumphs inform your work in ways you never thought possible. You're a better writer now than you were last week, not to mention last year, or last decade.

Your writing cares nothing for your cranky back. But as long as your faculties hold out, you can write. And writing can help your faculties hold out. **Such a deal!**

Who told the stories in
your family? Why them?

"Some want to write, others want to have written."

—variously attributed

Today-Only Writer's Special

Do not wish yourself anywhere but here: your life will unfold, your command of craft will evolve, your subjects will come and go. Whatever you are writing now, don't wish it away.

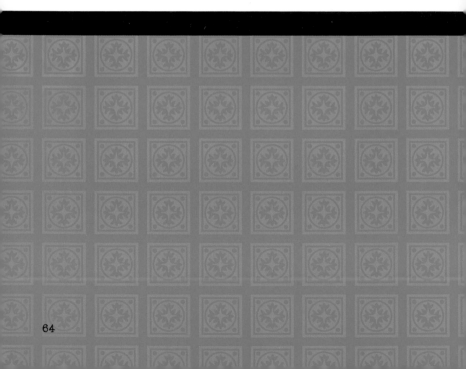

"The single biggest reason I got my stories taken in various literary magazines—and I want to stress this— is because I refused to give up. Period."

—Steve Almond,
author of *The Evil B.B. Chow*,
in an interview at wordriot.org

How many times in the average year do you say to someone you love,

"Don't give up."
"I know you can do this."
"These things take time."
"Be patient."

{ How many times do you say these same things to yourself? }

Write about the last time you
jumped to the wrong conclusion.

Write about a
glad-handing blowhard
who meets his match.

"Many [of today's young writers] seem to think senti-
mentality is a literary sin. I support writing programs,
but one unfortunate side effect is a cool, detached
tone—technically excellent stories with unclear emo-
tional centers. ... The writers miss their own feelings
because they fear stepping over the line. I think it's
better to step over the line than never get near it.

—Richard Russo,
author of *Empire Falls*, in an
interview with the *Seattle Weekly*

I had to smile when I read this quote from Richard Russo—
could he sound any less hip? But he's right, you know. A worse
literary sin than sentimentality, in my book, is indifference.
Go ahead: get your face dirty, sink all the way into the muck,
cry and wail and gnash your teeth. *Feel it*, for God's sake. You
can always pull back in revision, but if you don't wade all the
way in you'll never find the mud and monsters that your story
wants you to find. It's perfectly OK to love your characters
more than they love themselves.

Like the wolf that circles three times before bedding down, savvy writers choose their spot with care. They inhabit a unique physical space that reflects their current projects, long-term interests, and working style.

Whether your writing area resembles an empty chapel or a sidewalk tag sale, it should offer you comfort, privacy, motivation, and sources of information. If you need a nudge, here's your starter kit:

❶ a bookshelf
❷ a decent chair and a desk or table that fits your height
❸ a bulletin board and dry-erase board
❹ comfort books: novels, poems, stories, or essays you love
❺ at least one dictionary, one thesaurus, and several grammar/ usage guides
❻ maps, atlases, and a book of historical timelines
❼ a good-luck object
❽ a beautiful notebook or journal
❾ excellent light
❿ something living and/or flowing: cat, goldfish (not in combination), flowers, tabletop fountain ... ahhh

Writing is hard,

but it's not as hard as, say, coal mining or underwater welding. I've been known to juice up my misery to make my profession seem more worthy. Well, I'm not miserable. Writing deprives me of certain things—steady income; daily colleagues; even, at times, the will to live—but the list of things my writing *gives* me is much longer. The best thing on that list is living in a state of continual suspense.

{ In a writing life, things are always about to happen. }

Most human systems—families, companies, clubs, apartment buildings, political movements, governments, theater productions—include one key person without whom the whole thing would probably collapse.

Write about a
human system whose
key person has
just checked out.

A Wordsmith's Warm-up

Dump some Scrabble tiles into
a jar. Choose ten tiles and start
making words. Within minutes you
should have a decent jump-start.

FAQ #2

How do I get an agent?

Getting an agent these days takes more perseverance than the average person possesses. The average *writer*, however, knows from perseverance.

Start the old-fashioned way: find a connection. You might have a friend with an agent, or a doting teacher who might offer an introduction. Don't be hurt if your teacher or friend turns you down; writers often have rickety relationships with their agents and get understandably chary about wearing out their welcome.

Barring a good connection, hit the stacks: your local bookstore or library will have reference books that list agents. Scan the acknowledgments in books that remind you of yours—writers usually give their agents a nod. Get on the Internet, search "literary agents" or "lists of agents" and see what comes up. The Association of Authors' Representatives Web site (www. aar-online.org) lists agents by their area of interest and includes tons of links. There are also a few generous souls online whose blogs and sites chronicle their own attempts to get agents. Along with blog-clog, which can be entertaining but not necessarily helpful, you get a lot of contact information and even some sample rejection letters to let you know what to expect from certain agencies—which *is* helpful. Keep Googling and you'll find buckets of stuff. Start with everyonewhosanyone.com.

Once you've identified a few possibilities, make contact. I got my agent by sending a letter in which I mentioned that one of her clients suggested we might be a good match. I sent two short stories (always include return mailer and postage) with my query letter in the naive belief that an agent would be delighted to send out short stories to magazines on my behalf. She told me to get back to her when I had a novel to sell, so I did—three years later. **We've been together ever since.**

Write about the one thing you
never mentioned about that trip.

Today-Only
Writer's Special

*Ask for feedback from
someone who will shellac
you with the truth.*

Here's an exercise in precision that my sister Anne, who was my high school English teacher, used to assign:

Define and describe
a common object in 20
words or less.

toothpick
chair
sweater
pair of dice
double boiler

{ She gave me my one and only B
in English. Not that I'm bitter. }

Write about someone
who misinterprets
a compliment.

If your main character
is eluding you, have her write
a letter to the editor.

What's on her mind?

Write about finally giving in.

Memo From the Department
of Guilt and Satisfaction

For the first two years of his sojourn in my home, my cat Sonny—independent thinker, world-class shedder—vomited every day. Every. Single. Day. That's a lot of paper towels and upholstery cleaner. I tried special allergy food (at one point I was shelling out a buck-fifty a pop for small cans of minced rabbit), steroid shots, even acupuncture (long story, not my idea). Then, come spring, a brainstorm: no hair, no hairballs. Off to the groomer with him! Poor Sonny came back looking like a French poodle. They even left a pompon at the end of his tail. But it worked: I'm cleaning up vomit twice a week now instead of twice a day.

Back when Sonny sported a full coat and a dazzling repertoire of vomiting styles—regurgitating food, coughing up gerbil-sized hairballs, spewing lakes of bile—I often wished him a peaceful death in his sleep. But now I like him so much better. He looks fetching in his hairless suit, and in his yearning for warmth has become the lapcat I wanted from the get-go. I felt awful about clipping him—surely he was mortified—and yet I will do it again, because what I gain is, in my estimation, worth more than what he loses.

I confess this by way of reminding writers that in even the most innocuous human endeavors lie conflicting motivations and unanticipated results. While building your characters, be alert to what they give versus what they take, what they want versus what they expect, what they intend versus what they do, what they control versus what controls them. Reversal, irony, and detour is the stuff of human striving. And human striving is the one great subject that our writing always addresses.

Second Follow-up Notice
From the Department of
Procrastination Prevention

Three words: bowl of chips.
One sentence, one chip.

From the journal of Mary Ann Evans, aka George Eliot

1 January 1873: At the beginning of December, the eighth and last book of *Middlemarch* was published. ... No former book of mine has been received with more enthusiasm ... and I have received many deeply affecting assurances of its influence for good on individual minds. Hardly anything could have happened to me which I could regard as a greater blessing, than the growth of my spiritual existence when my bodily existence is decaying.

—from *Selections from George Eliot's Letters*,
Gordon S. Haight, editor

Don't you love this touching admission, this unabashed joy that George Eliot expresses over the admiration of others for her work? Remember, in your dark hours, that your creative work can soothe your bodily existence. Sometimes it's the only thing that can.

As a favor to my nephew Jeffrey, I once listened to an entire CD of one of his beloved hip-hop artists. Not surprisingly, I hated it, but it wasn't as excruciating as I expected. To be honest, I found the phrasing kind of fascinating, and discovered a line or two that caught my attention.

When was the last time you read something by an author you'd normally avoid? If you're twenty, ask for a recommendation from your grandmother. If you're sixty, read the last thing your son or niece or grandchild read. Suspend, for the moment, your cynicism and resistance: read the whole poem, the whole story, the whole essay, the whole novel.

{ Can this author give you something you didn't expect—even the tiniest pearl? }

Write in the voice
of someone talking
absurdly fast.

Why the big hurry?

Top Three Tips for Staving Off Writerly Despair

❶ Avoid the ones who expect you to fail.

❷ Avoid the ones who expect you to fail.

❸ Avoid the ones who expect you to fail.

I like to houseclean, and I'm well aware of house-
cleaning as metaphor. If you want to know how my
writing is going, drop by unannounced. If the stove
top has been freshly degunked, then the novel has
hit a potentially fatal snag and I'm wallowing in
disappointment. If the furniture's been moved, disappointment is sliding toward existential anguish.

What are your daily metaphors? How could
a stranger gauge your internal weather? If
all else fails you today, write about that.

Today-Only
Writer's Special

*Turn off your computer
and reintroduce
yourself to a pen.*

A Word on Silence

I write in silence, but silence is relative. Hailstorms and sonic booms barely register on my consciousness, but if the e-mail dinger goes off on my computer it's like being woken by the Four Horsemen of the Apocalypse.

Noise of the e-mail dinger type—that is, noise that rips you from your thoughts because a human being seeks your attention—is a writing killer. I include in this category music with lyrics, anything on television, squabbling children, beggar dogs, and cell phones, including all their attendant gizmos.

Most writers will tell you of lines, phrases, sometimes entire novels "popping" into their heads. If you're half listening to something else—or, worse, half listening *for* something else—you run the risk of missing the "pop."

Memo From the Department of Faking It

I once spent a delightful three days visiting my friend Cynthia in the tiny French town where she was living with her French boyfriend, Philippe. At the time, my first novel had been published in the States to the sound of utter silence. Cynthia and Philippe had a little party in my honor, so that I could meet their friends and practice my French. Little by little, over the course of the evening, I managed to glean, through my paltry understanding of their rapid-fire slang, that the party guests thought themselves in the company of an American luminary, a famous writer, a household name. They jokingly asked if I would put them in my next book, even though at the time I believed there would be no next book, ever. Because I lacked the vocabulary to convey the unglamourous truth, I simply smiled, said "*d'accord*," and played along. I've always felt a little guilty—but not too guilty—about my single evening of international fame and glory.

> Moral of the story: If you act like a star, they think you're a star.

If there exists out there a happy story of a writer resurrecting old, unfinished work and fashioning it into something new and successful, I haven't heard it. Even work that's only a couple of years old seems irretrievable to me. And sometimes, when I see my students reaching back through the misty years (to the stuff they wrote in college, usually), I want to grab their hands and beg them to stop. Retrieving an old subject, one that still haunts you, will work only if you begin afresh without looking back. Otherwise, you will waste your energy troubleshooting some other writer's work—*because you are no longer that writer.*

Wish your early work well. Do not scorn it. Be generous to the younger you who wrote it. This was the best you could do; be glad that you can now do better. Then say goodbye to that work, and begin something that the younger you would not have attempted.

"*I almost always give fiction as gifts and that's what I hope to receive, too.*"

– Margot Livesey,
from a Barnes and Noble interview

Aside from the cash output, there's no downside to book buying: You get to frequent your local bookstore, support your writing brethren (and sistren), and then, when you're finished reading, you get to keep the book forever, donate it to your local library or school or shelter, resell it to a used bookstore, or read it again.

Books last longer than candy and they're cheaper than flowers.

Say it with books.

"When I get a little money, I buy books. And if there is any left over, I buy food."

—Desiderius Erasmus,
Dutch thinker and humanist (1466-1536)

At this writing, a hardcover book costs about the same as

- one leg of a pair of jeans
- tie-rod ends for an ATV (parts only)
- one upscale-restaurant steak
- one-fourth of a ticket to a professional basketball game
- one-third of a haircut in a frou-frou salon
- one off-off-off-off Broadway (think Hoboken) ticket to *Waiting for Godot*

A paperback book costs about the same as

- one 12-pack of decent beer
- one tube of lipstick
- three vente lattes at Starbucks
- a modest meal for two at McDonald's
- two jugs of crystal-style cat litter, on sale
- one CD of Slim Whitman's greatest hits

{ If we don't buy the books, who will? }

If your main character had a different job, would his story change? If not, then the job is probably window-dressing on your part. Think carefully about what a job does to a character. If he's a dog groomer, then he probably refers to dogs by breed and thinks of animals as furry people. If he's a machinist, he knows the difference between a rack and a pinion and likes precision. If he's a second-grade teacher, he either likes or dislikes children, and undoubtedly has opinions about child-rearing, school politics, and classroom hamsters. Creating the illusion of inside knowledge enriches your characterizations and therefore your story.

Some Tips on Titles

No name yet for your baby? Herewith, a subjective primer on titles:

The best titles, in my view, contain a noun—not an abstract noun like *gratitude* or *restitution*—but a concrete noun like *blanket* or *avenue*. Often, the noun has a modifier: *The Lovely Bones* (Alice Sebold), "The Enormous Radio" (John Cheever). Modified nouns put an image in the reader's head, along with a mystery. Think *The Virgin Suicides* (Jeffrey Eugenides). Think *The Bluest Eye* (Toni Morrison). Think *Bee Season* (Myla Goldberg).

Verb forms make for less interesting titles. One of my early short stories, "Disappearing," holds my worst title ever. Verb forms strike me as too thematic, too calculated to announce the story's intentions. Titles like "Leaving Home," "Telling Lies," or "Wanting In" don't grab me because they give me no image. *Waiting* (Ha Jin) is a terrible title, if I may be so bold; *War Trash* (also Ha Jin) is great. Verbs work nicely in the imperative, though: *Come to Me* (Amy Bloom), *Read This and Tell Me What It Says* (Manette Ansay), *Say It* (Roland Flint).

Possessives give titles fizz because they relay an air of expectation: *The Pilot's Wife* (Anita Shreve), *The Bigamist's Daughter* (Alice McDermott), *Portnoy's Complaint* (Philip Roth).

Complete sentences sometimes make for weird and intriguing titles: *I Get on the Bus* (Reginald McKnight) is simple and inviting; "Everything That Rises Must Converge" (Flannery O'Connor) is forbidding and mysterious; *And Now You Can Go* (Vendela Vida) conveys both captivity and release.

And then, of course, there are the titles I love just because: *For Whom the Bell Tolls*, *Middlemarch*, *Franny and Zooey*, *Anne of Green Gables*, *One Flew Over the Cuckoo's Nest*. Some titles have zing, some … don't.

One last thing about titles: The right one often arrives late in the process, when you finally "get" what you're writing about. What a feeling!

> *"But I have never done my voracious reading to plan, and there are terrible holes in my literary knowledge that I dread will be accidentally revealed."*
>
> —Suzanne Lipsett,
> *Surviving a Writer's Life*

Don't you just adore Suzanne Lipsett for her honesty here? Most writers I know are brilliantly well read ... or so I surmise. Might they think the same of me? Well, then, I shall confess here: when it comes to literary holes, I've got some doozies. For example, I have never read one word of William Faulkner. There are other, even more mortifying gaps, but I'm hoping for a long life in which to rectify my failures. Presently I'm plugging a few holes with some Thackeray. I would just as soon discover the classics now anyway, when I'm old enough to truly understand them.

Write about a
fragile connection.

Because novels take so infuriatingly long to write and often require the writer to take vacations from them, they are prone to continuity errors, e.g., it's August at the beginning of the fictional day and July at the end. I've started annotating my scenes, e.g.: "Chapter 7; April; morning; scorching hot; Ona's point of view." Annotating makes resuming the work after a hiatus so much easier.

Write about
something
useless
and
beautiful.

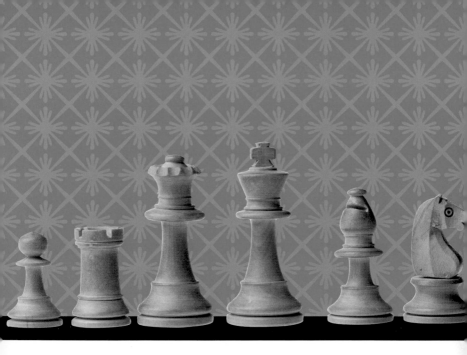

A Tip on Structure

Do you compartmentalize your characters (either real or fictional)? Does one character make his entrance, say his piece, then quiet down as the next character enters and does likewise? For example, the first scene shows little Jimmy being humiliated by his teacher, Mr. Bloom. Scene two shows little Jimmy trudging home, worrying about how to tell high-strung Mom. Scene three shows Jimmy telling Mom. Scene four shows the parent-teacher conference in which Jimmy's Mom confronts Mr. Bloom.

This is a sanitized, accessible, easy way to put together a story, but it doesn't make for much dramatic tension. Whenever possible, go for a higher body count in each scene. What if Jimmy tells on Mr. Bloom as Mom is picking him up in the classroom at the end of the school day? Now you've got three characters in conflict—let the sparks fly.

Work the following elements into a single scene:

a frightened animal

a civic leader

a small audience

"Much of the joy I always feel on the island lies pre-cisely in being free of the nagging suspicion I used to have that no matter what I was doing I might better be doing something else: if playing with my kids I should be working, if working I was neglecting my friends, if out with my friends I belonged home with my kids. How often I accused myself of reading when I should be writing, of writing when I ought to be reading, of staying indoors when I ought to be out in the streets ... filling my ears with oughts, but never knowing which ear the devil was whispering in."

—Alix Kates Shulman,
from *Drinking the Rain*

I came across this quotation as I was starting this book and working on a novel at the same time, feeling guilty about one whenever I worked on the other. *Ping!* went Shulman's words in my head.

One of the joys of writing is that sense of suspended time. Don't let the devil whisper in your ear! Whatever you are writing today, bask in that—and only that.

Revisit a story you've
told many times. Now,
tell a different story,
beginning with the thing
that happened after
the story's end.

In my writing workshops,

I see a lot of fresh, original student manuscripts, but I also get my share of stories that fall into recognizable categories. In *Making Shapely Fiction*, his delightful classic for beginning writers, the late Jerome Stern cautions against certain story types that are inexplicably irresistible to beginning writers.

Zero to One Hundred: In this story, the character undergoes an immense, fundamental, and utterly implausible transformation of character.

Zero to Zero: The character goes through the convolutions of the plot without changing one iota. Everything you know about him at the end (he's a cad, he's a loser, he's a greedy-guts; he's a swell guy) you already knew at the beginning.

The Banging Shutter: The story leads the reader through a series of scary plot turns, but in the end, the source of the perceived menace turns out to be something benign.

I would add the following titles to this list:

All My Trials, Lord: In this story, the writer heaps more misery on his character than God dreamed up for poor Job. (Alternate title: *Job Squared*.) There is no character development, just a lot of plot piled onto a lot of plot.

Six of One: Closely related to *All My Trials*, this story comes with a weight problem. All the characters' problems weigh the same. A's been diagnosed with cancer, B's mother died, C's boss just fired her. Or: A can't find her lipstick, B has no date for the prom, C got a B-minus in calculus. The story cannot find a shape because everything in it feels equally important, or equally trivial.

99 Bottles of Beer on the Wall: In this one, the writer devises an intractable plot structure, usually a countdown to a specific climax: minutes until the bomb goes off, days until the soldier comes home, hours until the birthday boy discovers his surprise. "Day Ten," or "06:59:03" goes the first line, beginning a countdown that seems like a good idea until the story becomes twice as long as it ought to be.

FAQ #3

How do I contact an agent?

With a query letter. My agent is one of the best in the business, and I'm lucky to have her. Here's a paraphrase of what she told me to tell you:

❶ The query should be either a brief letter with two additional pages, one for the synopsis of the book and one for your publishing credits and/or other intriguing information; or a somewhat longer letter that includes the synopsis, credits, and intriguing info in the body of the letter. (By "intriguing" she means anything related to you *as the author of this particular manuscript* that might make a marketing rep take notice: maybe you're the former Secretary General of the UN, or you climbed Everest without a Sherpa, or you're ninety-seven years old, or you researched your book in Siberia, or you come from Alabama with a banjo on your knee.) Ask if the agent would like to see all or part of the manuscript.

❷ The query should be concise, well written, and not self-aggrandizing. Make your book sound interesting, but do not brag. Do not cast the movie. Do not say, "This is your next bestseller!"

❸ If you have been recommended by a client of that agent, say so. If you specifically admire certain clients of that agent, say so.

❹ Do your homework. You'll be more appealing if you show that you understand the kind of book the agent usually represents. (In other words, don't send your children's poetry to an agent who specializes in adult commercial nonfiction.)

❺ Agents vary in opinion on whether to send part of the manuscript up front, with the query. (My agent thinks it's OK.) Keep in mind that many agents don't like e-mail queries.

❻ If you are sending part of a manuscript, don't send non-consecutive chapters.

❼ Enclose a self-addressed return mailer with sufficient postage.

My nephew Dan once said to my cat,
who was innocently napping in an armchair,

"Get a job."

Write about a pet with a job.

"Unless something has gone disastrously wrong,
other people aren't that interesting to write about."

—Margaret Atwood, in *Mother Jones*

Stories are always about trouble, but trouble comes in different guises.

It can be obvious:

- the family dog bites the tax collector
- an assassination ruins the peace accord

It can be unexplained:

- someone's been leaving strange drawings on the CEO's desk
- a son asks his mother for a $50,000 loan

It can be disguised as good fortune:

- a woman wins a new house ... that's haunted
- a struggling couple wins the lottery ... and gets sued by greedy relatives

While we're on the subject, remember that in a short story, the trouble should come sooner rather than later. The best short stories—even long ones—are wonders of economy. In a novel you have room to window-dress for a chapter or two, because the reader's expectations are different for a novel. In a short story, if the trouble (or at least the suggestion of trouble) isn't present by the end of the first page or two, your reader is gone.

Write about a library that runs out of books, a school
that runs out of children, a circus that runs out of animals.

What on earth happened?

How did your parents meet?

"I started writing Brick Lane *in July 2001, the day after my grandfather's funeral. We went on holiday, and it was a really nice sunny day and I felt that I couldn't put off writing any longer. My husband took the kids outside and I drew the curtains and I started writing that day. I think there is something quite galvanizing about a funeral that means you shouldn't keep putting things off."*

—Monica Ali,

author of *Brick Lane*, interviewed by

Neela Sakaria in *Bookwire*

Final Notice From the Department of Procrastination Prevention

Oh, that galvanizing feeling when a piece of writing insists on being born! The trouble—writer's block, inertia, terror—comes *after* that first rush of urgency. What do we do when the writing gets to a spot that requires something quite different from the initial push? Perhaps we have to shoulder into a tedious stretch of research, or a thorough examination of a part we're already bored with, or an interview with someone who makes us nervous.

My sister has a nifty system for accomplishing unloved tasks (calling the dentist, making a will, taking down the storm windows) that works equally well for writing. She simply picks a day on the calendar—two days or two months hence, depending—and when the day comes, she sees the thing written there and lo, it must be done, so she does it. The beauty of this system is that she doesn't worry about the loathsome task until its day arrives, freeing her up to ... you know, worry about other stuff.

Mark your writing task on a calendar—a complicated scene, a tricky timeline, a hard revision—and don't give it a single fretful second until its predetermined time arrives.

A Wordsmith's Warm-up

Haiku works sometimes.
You write these cryptic verses
Until something cracks.

Follow-up Memo From the Department of Just Showing Up

Every time you forgo writing for anything else—either worthy (your wedding) or unworthy (a rerun of *Law and Order*)—the words you would have written in that time disintegrate into the Black Hole of the Unattempted. Even if you had written nothing in those forty minutes you spent scrolling through blogs instead, you've still lost something valuable, because your Writing Nothing time is essential to building up to the Writing Something time.

I tell my students to sit in front of the blank page for a prescribed period every day, whether words arrive or not. Trust that you are not wasting your time. Quite the contrary: you're establishing a habit that will rescue you, time and again, when something else asks for your precious attention.

Addendum From the Department of Procrastination Prevention

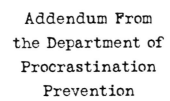

*When asked for a solution
to writer's block, the
poet William Stafford is
reported to have said:*

*"I just lower my standards
and keep on going."*

Two-Word Story Shake-up

Change a **"thank you"** to a
"screw you" and see what happens.

"I started writing [short stories] because I didn't have time to write any-thing else—I had three children. And then I got used to writing stories, so I saw my material that way, and now I don't think I'll ever write a novel."

—Alice Munro,
from a *New York Times* interview

How do you see *your* material? Is it a result of circumstance, or a fulfillment of your heart's desire? Alice Munro seems to have turned one into the other. Her kids are long gone but the short story still calls her. Perhaps she wanted to be a novelist once, but her life did not make the room, so she accommodated. Have you made a similar peace with circumstantial limitations, or are you fighting a battle you can't win?

{ Spend an hour today writing about writing—yours. }

Write about the first day
of your last job.

———————⟫⟩•0•⟨⟪———————

Write about the last day
of your first job.

What if you
finally did what
you've always
wanted to do?

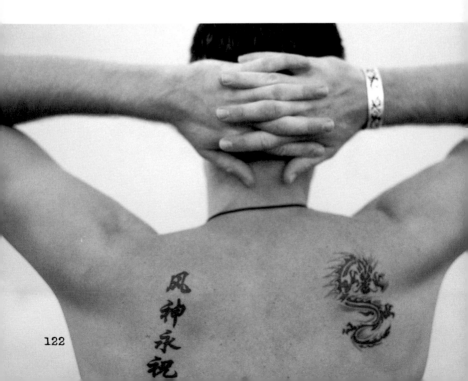

Write about an immigrant
who refuses to be noble,
humble, or dignified—

from the point of
view of her husband.

Are all your characters
reasonably attractive?

{ Ugly someone up and start anew. }

Write about stinginess
disguised as generosity.

The last *New Yorker* cartoon that made me laugh out loud depicted a cheerful bird in a Grim Reaper outfit landing on some poor guy's window sill. The caption read, "Hi! I'm the bluebird of death."

Think of a familiar trope that could use some shaking up. How about the Mild, Mild West? The Cesspool of Eden? Prince Obnoxious? Make a list and run with it.

Write about the
ELEPHANT
in the room.

Other people's dreams are boring.

Unless we're in them. A dream as a story device works too often as a cheap shortcut to the hard work of storytelling. Perhaps we have a character who is afraid of his own success. Instead of allowing this character to reveal his fear by interacting with other characters and events, we add a dream sequence in which the character burns himself at the stake using old copies of his résumé as kindling. What, then, becomes of the story? The device itself swaggers onto center stage and shouts at the audience, leaving the story lurking in the wings.

Ask yourself: What am I trying to reveal here that I have failed to reveal through good old-fashioned character development? Don't allow an easy story device to rob you of the great pleasure of plotting your way into your character's psyche.

A Few Words About Words

Have you sorted out these commonly misused words?

Convince means to get someone to change her mind; *persuade* means to get someone to take an action. (You can convince a kid that broccoli is healthy, but can't persuade him to eat it.)

Tortuous means winding—a tortuous path, stairway, or logic. *Torturous* connotes torture—a torturous root canal, bar exam, or surprise party.

Imply means to suggest or indicate; *infer* means to conclude or assume. On this page I *imply* that words should be used as precisely as possible. My readers might *infer* that I'm a grumpy old stickler.

Comprise refers to the whole, not the parts. Think of it as a synonym for "include": the USA comprises fifty states; the committee comprises seven people; the schoolyard comprises seven play areas. People often use it, incorrectly, in the passive voice, i.e., "is comprised of," but that's exactly like saying "is included of." Instead, try "is composed of fifty states," or "is made up of seven play areas."

Flaunt means to show off something in an obvious, even vulgar manner; *flout* means to scorn or defy something. You *flout* the rules if you ignore all your parking tickets. You don't, however, *flaunt* the rules—you flaunt a new car, a designer dog, or your superior knowledge of easily confused words.

Write about the
first time you conversed
with a stranger.

A Primer on Structure

Many of us think of "plot" and "structure" as interchangeable terms. Though a good plot does have a structure—most fundamentally, a beginning, a middle, and an end—plot is merely one element of a much larger composition.

Think of structure as the alliance of three major elements: plot, story, and design.

Plot is the easy part: you just follow your nose. Plot is the "what happens next." Character A goes to the store, has a spat with Character B over the last bottle of Sizzle-Snazzle nail polish, the bottle gets broken, Character A is ordered from the store in disgrace.

Story is the hard part: you discover it through irony, juxtaposition, nuance, metaphor, all the things that make prose worth reading. Story provides subtext, motivation, insight into the character's morality. As the dustup over the Sizzle-Snazzle unfolds, Character A wrestles with her humiliating financial situation, unintentionally reveals her sense of entitlement, ditches her belief in the goodness of others, and resurrects a long-dormant prejudice against people like Character B. Story is the part that emotionally engages your reader by revealing universal truths that illuminate the human condition. *Plot* is what happens to the character, and *story* is what happens to the reader.

Design is the fun part. It's the sum of your technical decisions. Whose point of view? Which tense? Lots of dialogue or all narrative? Four lengthy sections or thirty-two short chapters? Strict chronology or liberal use of flashback?

In other words, structure comprises both plot and story and places them into a deliberate design.

A change to any one of these elements can cause the structure to collapse in part or in total. For example, what if we retain the *design* in the story of Cinderella—third person, chronological order, Cinderella as main character—but tweak the *plot* just a bit, turning wicked stepsisters to wicked stepbrothers? Suddenly we've got a different *story*: the brothers certainly aren't vying for Prince Charming's charms. Probably greed, not envy, bedevils them—which changes the *plot* (if they want Cinderella to get the prince and his money, the fairy godmother becomes moot), which changes the *story*, which may, after all, change the *design* we've tried to retain.

Much of our writerly frustration comes from the domino effect of changes to a single structural element. Recognizing and understanding those elements constitutes step one in winning back our equanimity.

"I'm forty-two, so I finally just decided, 'Well, if it turns out that the only thing you can do halfway decently is write stories, then you should just be grateful that you can even do that, and don't get all stupid about it and insist on writing a mediocre novel just so that you can say you've done it.'"

— George Saunders, author of *Pastoralia* talking to Booksense.com

Are you writing a novel because somebody told you stories don't sell? Do you write essays because poetry doesn't pay? Are you wasting your one and only life following somebody else's calling? Love of writing is nothing to trifle with. If you're supposed to be writing poetry, write it.

{ Save the novel for your next life —
unless you come back as a playwright. }

A Tip on Style

How many of your sentences perform double duty? A double-duty sentence gives the reader both information and suggestion. Examine this string of *single-duty* sentences:

> The boy entered the stranger's house. He looked around. On the mantel someone had arranged a collection of dog figurines. Several of them were chipped. Some of them had missing heads. The boy shivered, wondering if the person who lived here meant him harm. For the moment, he chose not to contemplate that.

Notice how each sentence conveys a single piece of information. The first establishes the boy entering the house; the second informs us that he's looking around; the third informs us that the mantel contains figurines; and so on. Try packing these sentences a little, combining information with suggestion, to both vary the prose and intensify the reader's experience. You often have to recast a sentence to allow it to perform double duty. Once you start revising this way, many single-duty sentences can be cut altogether. Notice also that one of the best ways to add suggestion is through imagery.

> The boy entered the stranger's house. On the mantel stood a collection of dog figurines lined up firing-squad style, several of them headless from a calamity the boy preferred not to contemplate.

In this version, most of the single-duty sentences are rendered unnecessary from the one suggestion-filled sentence that replaces them. The firing-squad image suggests potential for harm, conjuring the possibility that heads have been deliberately lopped off ... and that the hapless boy might be next in line.

Write about an outsider at a convention of fanatics: Trekkies, Barbie collectors, people named O'Malley, ferret fanciers, film critics ...

Write about a guessing game that goes wrong.

Follow-up Memo From the
Department of Attitude Adjustment

At the end of my most recent book tour—tired and ungrateful and
whiny—I was deservedly caught out by a young reporter from a small
paper who said to me, "Most of us would kill to get a book tour."
Touché, my friend. So I'll break from the tedious writers' tradition of
complaining about the book tour and tell these tales instead:

Portland, Maine: At Longfellow Books, my local bookstore,
we had 125 happy souls, excellent wine, and a cherry whipped-
cream cake that people will be talking about long after they've
forgotten my book.

Southern Massachusetts: In walked two girl cousins on whom I hadn't set eyes since we were all listening to The Monkees on LP. They looked exactly the same and turned out to be passionate readers. We had a joyful family reunion a month later.

Oxford, Maine: Five attendees. Chairs pulled into a circle. A crackling thunderstorm. Beautiful.

Bangor: A woman arrived with a dog that fit into her purse. The dog liked me.

Denver: A nice young man gave me an engraved bookmark to thank me for coming.

Mt. Desert Island: I got a cool canvas bag and big audience.

Bar Harbor: I sold lots of books and collected the following quotes, which I realize sound completely fake, but you'll just have to trust me on this. I wrote them on the back of a Harry Potter party flyer, and they kept me grinning on the three-hour drive home.

Quote #1: "Books, books, books! I love books!" said a portly old gal who looked over my wares, then cheerfully bought a tower of books—by other people.

Quote #2: "Can you show me the bathroom?"

Quote #3: "Look, Joey, that's an *author*. If you buy her book, she signs it, and then if she gets famous you can resell it for lots of money."

Here's an exercise I call Green Light/Red Light that works well in a group. Each group member writes two simple scenarios and places them in a jar. Once the entries are deposited, each member removes one entry, which will be the "green light," then a second entry, which will be the "red light." The object is to begin a story with the green-light prompt and end the same story with the red-light prompt, connecting two events in some imaginative way. Here's a list from one jar. Mix and match them any way you like. With luck, you might get the first draft of a story.

Green Light	Red Light
sudden trip	*clown school*
figure eights	*oil strike*
Fig Newtons	*17-year locusts hatching*
four babies	*a construction mishap*
obscene phone call	*a drunk and a missed train*
car trip	*an animal bite*
time capsule	*seven ribbons*
high fever	*solar eclipse*
ex-lovers	*free tickets*
an attack	*a haircut*
closed library	*translation problem*
world's smallest clock	*a plague on both their houses*
box of hair	*city in crisis*
tractor accident	*church renovation*
Osama bin Laden	*Sunday school*
a lie	*thirty-three candles*

Action is the essence of story.

Are your characters—or you, if you're writing non-fiction—too ruminative, reflective, pondering? Think action, from buying a muffin with the last of one's change, to chasing a loved one down a narrow street, to detonating a bomb. When a character acts, the reader engages.

Would you rather read about a man thinking about death, or a man building his own coffin?

Write about the last time you entered
a church—what brought you there?

{ If you're a regular churchgoer, write about the
last time you declined the spiritual realm. }

143

FAQ #4

Since getting an agent is so difficult and time-consuming, why shouldn't I approach a publisher on my own?

I can't think of a single big publishing house left that still accepts unagented submissions of any kind.

Small, independent presses are a slightly different story. They tend to publish "smaller" books—smaller sales, smaller print runs—but that doesn't mean smaller in quality. Go there if you're going alone. Your book of poems, your analysis of Hemingway's later works, or your impossible-to-categorize postmodern metafictional novella will be much more at home with a small press anyway. When it comes to knocking on the door, be sure to follow the protocol, because even the small presses are getting mighty prickly of late. (Almost nobody will take submissions electronically, for example.)

Some of my favorite books lately have come from small presses: *Warp & Weft*, a novel by Edward J. Delaney (The Permanent Press); *Curious Attractions: Essays on Fiction Writing* by Debra Spark (University of Michigan Press); *Reasons for Leaving*, stories by John Manderino (Academy Chicago Publishers); *And Give You Peace*, a novel by Jessica Treadway (Graywolf Press); *For the Beauty of the Earth: Birding, Opera, and Other Journeys*, essays by Thomas Urquhart (Shoemaker & Hoard).

Today-Only Writer's Special

Imagine—in full, horrific Technicolor—
that the first thing you ever wished to publish
had actually been published.

Write about

the day

before the

disaster.

Give this photograph a title.

Now tell the **story.**

148

Write about a journey with
an uncertain destination.

A Wordsmith's Warm-up

First sentence: one word;

    second sentence: two words;

        third sentence: three words;

            and so on, until you trick your way in.

Write as sympathetically as you can about someone who gives you the heebie-jeebies.

A Tip on Style

If your style tends toward the lyrical, then you probably employ a lot of similes. Similes give your reader a fresh way of looking at everything from people to prunes—or people who look like prunes—and instantly vivify your prose. Paradoxically, however, too many similes actually *deaden* the prose, because you end up with a surfeit of "like a this" and "as a that," giving the prose a slack, predictable quality.

Here's a trick for retaining the strong images you want without numbing the sentences: Whenever possible, change a key word of the simile (usually a noun) into another part of speech (usually an adjective). Examples:

*Lucretia petted the rottweiler's head, which felt as round and solid as a **turnip**.*

*Lucretia petted the rottweiler's solid, **turnip-shaped** head.*

(The noun "turnip" becomes part of a compound adjective in the second example.)

*Edgar's face was shaped something like a **cat's**.*

*Edgar's vaguely **feline** face came into view.*

(The noun "cat" becomes the adjective "feline" in the second example. You could also use "catlike." Bonus: you also ditched the inert "was.")

152

*Living with Jerry felt like a ride on a cut-rate **roller coaster**.*

*In the fall, I found myself **roller-coastering** toward another year with Jerry.*

(The noun "roller coaster" becomes a verb in the second example.)

When you hide some of your similes in this fashion, then the traditionally constructed ones that remain pack more of a punch:

Singing "The Twelve Days of Christmas," Sister Frances sounded like six geese a-laying.

Three-Word Story Shake-up

Change "I love you" to "Tell the truth" and see what happens.

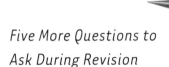

Five More Questions to Ask During Revision

❶ Does this draft have a beginning, middle, and end?
❷ Do scenes flow logically from one to another?
❸ Is there a missing scene?
❹ Is the ending too rushed or, to the contrary, too slow?
❺ Does the ending leave you with too many questions to be able to say what the piece is about?

How many words for sounds (bing, bang, boom; thwup, thwip, thwap; yap, yip, yawp) *can you come up with in a minute? Set your timer and fire away.*

{ Pick the best of the lot and write about the source of that sound. }

Write about two people trying
to fit into a space (physical or
metaphorical) meant for one.

Today-Only Writer's Special

Tell your loved ones to kindly get out of your face.

Write about someone who
accidentally destroys
something irreplaceable.

A Tip on Structure

How do we revise a flawed piece when we can't quite pin down the trouble? For a revealing look at a troublesome narrative, try taking the thing apart scene by scene in order to examine how each part serves—or detracts from—the whole.

The exercise is deceptively simple: all you do is count your scenes. This nitty little process can give you some useful information, not the least of which is how you define a scene. Usually a scene ends with a change—of characters (someone exits or enters) or setting (the story switches from the living room to the attic, or from Nyack to Rome, or from Bonnie's point of view to Clyde's point of view)—but you don't have to get too picky here. You know when there's a shift in your story. That shift marks the end of one scene and the beginning of another.

Once you arrive at a number, examine what, if anything, this information tells you about where the story has gone wrong. Some possible revelations:

• What if you count ten scenes in an eighteen-page narrative? Might you be trying to cram too much plot into too small a space, or sacrificing character development to relentless action?

• What if, by contrast, you find only two long scenes in a similar space? Might the piece be suffering from a surfeit of reflection, recollection, and rumination—i.e., too much talk and not enough action?

• What if you can't delineate the piece by scene? Possibly the piece is still in the exploratory stage when you're

searching for your subject rather than writing about it. The piece might be much farther away from its final form than you thought.

Or not. Only you can make these decisions about your own piece, but by putting it through these paces you can at least clarify what kind of decisions have to be made. Intense scrutiny of form forces you to write with more intention. We all hope for the perfect form to arrive by intuition, and sometimes—sweet mother of Jeremiah!—it does. But you can't make a body of work out of happy accidents. Sooner or later you have to burrow deep into craft and tunnel through the gravel just like every wretched scribe who ever preceded you. And you will feel the same gratifying sense of purpose and accomplishment that they did.

Write about the first one to quit.

"First were the poems that were wild, melodramatic tales, like Alfred Noyes' 'The Highwayman,' or were simply fun, like James Whitcomb Riley's 'Little Orphan Annie.' In some real way I am leery of that emphasis 'great poetry' because I haven't the least idea whether these poems [I loved as a boy] were such, then or now."

—Robert Creeley, author of *For Love: Poems 1950-1960* (among many other volumes), from an interview in the *Cortland Review*

If Robert Creeley refuses to define "great" literature, then maybe the rest of us should take notice. Why not simply love what we love, guard our desire, and write the books we want to read? All the anointing and designating should reside in a place safely outside the realm where we labor over our work, one precious word at a time, with no thought but for the writing at hand.

Today-Only
Writer's Special

Write what
you don't know.

Write about a delivery that goes astray.

*This one comes courtesy of
teacher and writer Alfred dePew ...*

Start with
the day
that was
different.

Write about one
person pressured
into persuading
another person
to do something
dangerous.

Write about what got
left behind on purpose.

Write about what got
left behind by accident.

Write about a meeting
that goes on so long it
becomes something other
than a meeting.

Write about
a beautiful evening
ruined by
a bad joke.

"Anybody who believes two black people agree on any-thing ought to visit a barbershop in Harlem sometime."

—James McBride, author of *The Color of Water: A Black Man's Tribute to His White Mother*, interviewed at powells.com

McBride is referring here to how tempting it is to make certain types of characters—real or fictional—play to type. If no two black people agree on anything, the same goes for white people, CEOs, single mothers, Iranians, underage girlfriends, tourists, baseball players, and illegal aliens. Examine your characterizations for those facile strokes that generalize rather than humanize your characters. If your casino owner, named Carlo, likes sloe gin and fast women, so be it, but he'd better be aware of his own stereotype. And unless you've got a really good reason to name his hooker girlfriend Tiffany and give her the proverbial heart of gold, she's going to seem a lot more human if you name her Ethel and grant her a more complicated temperament.

Write about a painful loyalty.

Take an ordinary object (a corkscrew, a clothespin, a bookmark) and list all the ways it might be used beyond its intended purpose—or even in opposition to its intended purpose. I'm thinking of my neighbor, who once shooed a cat from her dooryard by flapping a **welcome** mat.

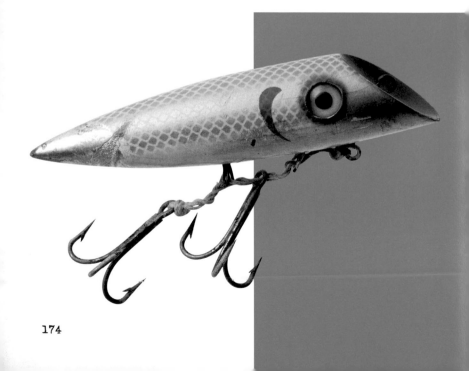

A Wordsmith's Warm-up

Type or hand-copy, verbatim, a
favorite scene from a writer you
greatly admire. This fascinating
exercise gives you a visceral sense
of how the scene is constructed
and why it works. No matter how
many times you've read the passage, you'll discover something
you never noticed.

"People make a lot of assumptions about the art of writing for children, almost all of them false. They assume that because the form is short, it's easy. (Poetry is also short, but if anything that makes it harder.) They assume that children want to be provided with a moral at the end. (Grown-ups don't want their books to read like a church sermon, so why would children?) They assume that if an event really happened, it will make a great story. That it's better if it rhymes. And so on. What they really should assume is that a children's book needs interesting characters, a compelling plot, and a satisfying ending—just like any other book."

—Amy MacDonald, author of *Little Beaver and the Echo, Cousin Ruth's Tooth, No More Nice,* and a dozen other books for children.

Words About Words

The English language is so vast, so nuanced, so colorful and everchanging that it requires a lexicon of words just to describe itself and its users. Here are some of my favorites:

synecdoche (syn-ECK-doe-key): a figure of speech in which the part stands in for the whole, or the whole stands in for the part, e.g., "I left town with the law on my tail." The *law* stands for *police officer* and *tail* stands for *my whole self.*

malonym: a metaphor, cliché, or popular expression mangled by a sound-alike mistake, e.g., "Eddie's daughter is pretty as a pitcher."

contronym: a word that is its own opposite, e.g., sanction (to endorse, to boycott), transparent (invisible, obvious), or handicap (to advantage, to disadvantage)

sesquipedalian: given to using long words

logophile: a word lover

Begin with the words:

 As long as I have you here ...

Write about the first guy in line.

Today-Only
Writer's Special

*Read the latest research
on life-expectancy rates.*

{ Translation: If you haven't published your first book by
the age of thirty, you've got about seventy years to go. }

Write about discovering
an unexpected vice
in someone you thought
you knew well.

FAQ #5
What's the protocol for approaching the smaller presses?

Publishing houses have varying guidelines; common sense and good manners will work with any house that doesn't publish specific submission guidelines. In other words, don't send all six hundred pages of your manuscript with a "To Whom It May Concern" salutation on a boilerplate cover letter.

Start with a letter addressed to an actual person. (Call the company and ask for a name if you can't find one.) Make your introductory letter concise and lucid, include a brief synopsis of your book, and enclose no more than one sample chapter or about twenty-five to thirty pages. If including a chapter, add a return mailer with sufficient postage.

Forewarned is forearmed, so herewith I present snippets from the submissions guidelines for some of the friendlier small presses:

Graywolf Press: Because we do not accept unsolicited manuscripts, we ask that you first send a query letter by regular mail.

Algonquin Books: If you would like us to consider your manuscript, please send a twenty-page sample of your work, a cover letter, and a self-addressed, stamped envelope.

Alice James Books: We are currently accepting submissions only through our two annual competitions.

Beacon Press: Please send us a letter of inquiry, a proposal, and a current CV.

Coffee House Press: CHP publishes emerging and midcareer authors. Nearly all CHP authors have had works published in literary magazines or other publications.

Persea Books: We take on poetry manuscripts very, very selectively.

In other words, it's a jungle out there, even in the small jungle. But you already knew that. Here you are anyway. **Carry on.**

Write about
the painting
beneath the
painting.

"I was trying for a long time to write my third novel in the first-person voice, and felt a sense of artistic duty, having written two third-person novels, to show that I could do a voice novel, a first-person novel. I wasted a lot of time—more than a year all together—trying to get that voice to work."

—Jonathan Franzen, talking about his (third-person) novel *The Corrections*, in *Poets & Writers* magazine

I like this quote because it illuminates the difference between the author's agenda and the agenda of the thing he is writing. If you find yourself locked in a similar death grip, it might help to think of your work as an entity that resides outside your ken, a thing with its own intentions. Those intentions may remain elusive for days, weeks—even years, alas. But if you think of your work as stronger than you, more stubborn than you, willing to hold out for as long as it takes until you accept what it wants to become—the process begins to make more sense. It feels like a struggle because it *is* a struggle. *The Corrections* wanted to be in the third person, so it fought Franzen's insistence until he finally got the message.

We fight our work so mightily because we prefer the path of least resistance. If we find present tense easier than past, or third person easier than first, then that's the path we take. Or we take the path of most resistance, as Franzen did, out of "artistic duty," aka artistic ego. Not until we've trotted quite a ways down that initially chosen path do we begin to wonder whether we've-ever-so-possibly made a mistake, but at this point we're so invested—in time, effort, emotion—that we can't summon the guts to double back and set a different course.

I'm guessing that Franzen knew within fifty pages that the first person wasn't going to work for the book that became *The Corrections*; but fifty pages represents a lot of grimly devoted days, so he soldiered on, ignoring that far-off whine, getting to, say, 150 pages, which of course made starting over even more objectionable, so he kept going ... and so on. Cutting our losses hurts—badly—but we can either do it earlier, when it's painful, or do it later, when it's just about unbearable.

Is your draft getting away from you because you're trying to do too much? A story—however many-faceted—is about one thing. An essay is about one thing. A poem is about one thing. Even a novel, which may range over many places, subjects, time frames, and characters, illuminates a single central theme. All the parts should serve the whole.

So, examine your draft and decide whether you're actually working on two separate drafts. If so, the good news is that you now have two stories or essays or poems to write instead of one; the bad news is that you have to work harder to get to the heart of each separate matter. Oh, wait.

{ That's the good news, too. }

Write about a family tradition that others might find odd.

The mother of one of my college friends used to let the family dog eat at the table, with a dinner plate and napkin—on Sundays. Another friend tells the story of her grandma washing, drying, and ironing dollar bills before giving them out as birthday presents.

Write about
a collection
that pleases one
person and
enrages another.

If everybody you know talks pretty much the same way, you gotta get out more. Listen for the idioms that make our beloved language so beefy and variable, so endlessly thrumming. My pal Ed refers to heavily pierced guys as **"tackle boxes."** My brother dismisses any food he hates as **"slumgullion."** My friend Amy coined the word **"mumchance,"** which means glum and thick-headed, an adjective that, now that I think about it, accurately describes **"glumgoblins,"** a noun I made up to refer to unrelenting naysayers. Oddball locutions honestly thrill me, and they often spark a voice that will in turn spark a character that will then ignite a story.

A Word on Irony

Irony gives writing an intangible hum, a zingy *je ne sais quoi* that assures your readers that by sticking with you they'll learn a thing or two about being human in an absurd world. Irony is hard to define but easy to spot. Think juxtaposition. Think reversal. Think incongruity, on a large scale (burning the village to save the villagers) or small (running out your computer battery while writing a piece on long-life computer batteries).

A rainstorm on your wedding day is plain bad luck.

A rainstorm on the weatherman's wedding day is ironic.

A child being mauled by the evil neighbor's dog is horrifying.

A child being mauled by his assistance dog is ironic.

A sleazy city councilor arrested under a new law is delicious.

A sleazy city councilor arrested under a new law that passed by one vote—his—is ironic. And delicious.

The next time you see
your mother, ask the
question you always
wanted to ask.

Are you haunted by a missing scene, something you're afraid to write because it's too hard, or too complicated, or beside the point, or too focused on another character? Write it anyway and find out what you're missing.

It might help to first write *about* the scene, with no thought toward making the prose anything but serviceable: "I avoided this scene because …"; "This scene scares me because …"; "What I think might be happening in this scene is … " Act as your own therapist, and go where you're afraid to go.

I have been asked why I teach writing, since statistics hold that 99 percent of the people to whom I teach the fundamentals of story writing will not actually publish a story. True, perhaps. But what an appalling criterion for teaching people to write with more intention, more craft, more delight. To write means to live thoughtfully. To respect your inner life. To engage with the world. Why shouldn't everyone aspire to this richness?

Publishing is something else altogether, and does not belong in the same sentence with the word writing.

Write about someone
working hard
toward a morally
ambiguous goal.

Write about a
found book that
changes everything.

*"In an immediate and very
human way it's about staying
power on the brink of disaster."*
— David McCullough, discussing
his book *1776* in bookreporter.com

Historian David McCullough is talking about
the stories of the American Revolution here,
but he's also describing every story through-
out human history that ever bore repeating.
Aren't we humans all about staying power on
the brink of disaster?

{ Look at the thing you're writing.
If there's no brink, add one. }

197

Three people.
A cold morning.
One vacant movie house.

Go.

Five More Questions to Ask Yourself During Revision

❶ Can you follow the emotional line of the piece? Does it make sense?

❷ What are the key moments in this draft? Are they given enough time?

❸ Is there something in this piece that resonates beyond itself? We're talking about universal truths here.

❹ Does the piece contain a rise and fall, or do all the events in the story get equal weight?

❺ Is the piece too obviously constructed—too true to a formula—to deliver an emotional wallop?

Memo From the Department of Self-Delusion

Of course I should have been thrilled: one of my short stories was selected to be part of a special radio broadcast. The event was to be held a few months hence at one of the coolest venues in New York City, at which time my story, paired with another by a writer I had long admired, would be read by a famous actor in front of a live audience of intelligent, presumably well-dressed aficionados of literature. The catch was that I had to cut three pages in order to fit the story to the format.

Three pages! Impossible, I thought, quite insulted, really; the story was only nineteen pages as it was. Did these people think I flung words willy-nilly without caring where they landed? Had they failed to notice how meticulously I plied my craft? The story had been published already, for crying out loud. The nerve of these people!

Then I read it. And felt even worse. For entirely different reasons.

Instead of the shimmering, inviolable thing I remembered, I found, to my dread and sorrow, *at least* three pages' worth of dross that could be dispatched without an instant's ceremony. *At least!* Out they went: a flabby passage here, two boring paragraphs of backstory there, a dozen sentences cut down to size. I did this not with satisfaction, but with a building sense of existential horror. Not horror for the lost pages—good riddance to that!—but horror over my own myopia, my self-delusion, my belief, a mere five years past, that the story I'd written was anything beyond merely decent. Adequate. Competently written. Holy saints in heaven, what was I *thinking*?

Well, I must have been thinking what we have to think when we do the best we can with what we've got. I thought my story was good. Insightful. Powerful, even. The best I'd written. How can I go on if I don't think that about the work at hand? Nonetheless, it is crushing indeed to meet up with one's limitations, especially after they've been put on display as something quite the opposite.

My husband said, "Can't you make just this one thing easy?" And so I shall try. I shall attend the gala event, act as if I belong there, and try to love listening to my own story being broadcast to people who like stories. Besides, I'm quite fond of the newly streamlined version. It's good. Insightful. Powerful, even. The best I've written.

"I'm compelled by language, so there are days for instance where if it sounds flat and dry I try to find something else to do that will help the book. That often means going to poets and reading poetry. That's my fuel tank."

—Alice Sebold, interviewed by Dave Weich at powells.com

What's in your fuel tank? Poetry? Weight lifting? Conversation? Dogs? Tea? Housework? Is the tank empty or full today? If it's empty, fill 'er up.

Write about a

**shocking
discovery**

(not a body)

in a fallow field.

FAQ #6

How do you know when a piece is done?

The infuriating answer to this one is, "You just *know*." The knowledge comes from the gut, at least for me. I know I'm finished when the unfocused sense of impending doom—the low-level anxiety that has accompanied almost every word of the story or novel or article or essay—magically disappears. There's a feeling that the story has resolved itself in some way, or at least reached a state of equilibrium, in which the ending fulfills the beginning. Another, less ambiguous clue is when I find myself changing things back to what they were a few days previous.

"Done" is a relative term anyway. Raymond Carver revised his great short stories even after they were published, and he's not the only one. Do you mean done for good, or done for now? The real question is this: "Is the piece finished, or just this version of it?"

Work a little magic with the following words:

gumballs   flimflammery

tootsie   short-timer

chummy

*Five Fab Questions
to Ask Your
Main Character*

❶ How did you get
your name?

❷ What object from
childhood do you
still own?

❸ What was in yester-
day's mail?

❹ When did you stop
being happy?

❺ What is your stron-
gest superstition?

Write a scene in which a woman, under no threat of bodily harm, is forced to empty her purse.

Memo From the Department
of Attitude Adjustment

Sometimes it really does seem as if everyone you know is more successful than you. Sometimes it's all in your head. And sometimes, alas, it isn't.

But while you're standing on a lower rung of the ladder of success, looking longingly upward, somebody on a rung lower still is gazing longingly up at you. Why, oh why, do we always gaze up? Why not gaze down once in a while? Is unhappiness merely a function of comparing ourselves to the wrong people?

Remember when your biggest goal was simply to begin? Just that? Go back there and look up again—**at yourself.**

If you have only a fuzzy idea of what your story is trying to tell you, try interpreting it as an image, as if you were designing the book cover. Grab a box of crayons and let fly. This pleasant exercise can sometimes bring disparate elements into a single focus.

Today-Only
Writer's Special

⟫⟩⊙⟨⟪

If you need help on your
writing path, ask for it.
If you don't need help at
the moment, help someone
else. Offer to read a manuscript, babysit a child,
listen to a tale of artistic
angst. We've all been there
and will be again.

⟫⟩⊙⟨⟪

A woman on a beach,
dressed in black, shouting
a single word to the ocean.

{ What is that word?
How did she come to this? }

"People sometimes say that the problem with writing from life, with using autobiographical material, is the instinct for veracity: we can't stop ourselves from being true to the experience, even when that sort of truth is no good for the story. The problem may actually be that a true story provides too much material; it doesn't leave enough out."

—Debra Spark, in her book *Curious Attractions: Essays on Fiction Writing*

I've watched enough students struggle with shapeless, over-stuffed, autobiographical "fiction" to understand completely what Debra Spark is getting at here. So, here's your task for today: Write down a family story you have always loved. Now, force yourself to cut it by one half—using the word counter on your processor if you must. Don't regret all those severed details. Instead, trust that their absence will allow the essence of the story to emerge.

Begin with
a smell
that brings
it all back.

Five Final Questions to Ask During Revision

❶ Is this really the final version, the one to which you'll be proud to attach your name? Or does it need a few weeks to settle before you pronounce it finished?

❷ Are you having second thoughts—even mild ones—about something in this piece that might embarrass or hurt another person?

❸ Does this piece belong to your apprenticeship, that is, something from which you learned a thing or two about craft, but which was never destined to be part of your public oeuvre?

❹ If this piece still isn't ready—and possibly never will be—can you set it aside, with gratitude, and begin the next one?

❺ Did you love the process as much as you love the outcome?

My friend Candice Stover, a poet from Mt. Desert, Maine, lives in a house filled with poetry. Literally, I mean: use her bathroom and you'll find a poem on the door, another above the sink. Draw some water from her kitchen tap and a poem appears at eye level; sit for some tea in the parlor and poems appear on the tea tables. Poems from poets you know and poets you don't. Political poems, nature poems, love poems, poems about political arrogance, about fathers, about humility in the face of disaster. Candice can quote vast numbers of poems by heart—and from the heart—for she sees not only her world but the world at large as a repository of poetic sensibility. Birthdays, death, elections, road construction, war, squirrels, grief, travel, weddings, rocks, shoes, love: there is no subject so great or so small for which a poem cannot offer clarity and meaning.

Every true poet I know, it seems, lives this way, in the gut-rock faith that words can light our way through the darkness and reveal meaning in existence. "I have no words for this," we say when life itself overwhelms us with grief or happiness. But we do have words, as it turns out: words for everything, if we wait for them, and search for them.

Je crois aux mots

Je crois que les mots sont des petits dieux

Je crois que les livres sont des bibles …

—from Ce que je crois by Marcel Pomerlo

This quote crossed my path on my last day in Quebec City, just as I was putting the final touches on this manuscript. It translates, "I believe in words; I believe that words are little gods; I believe that books are bibles."

I believe, too. Words, like gods, connect us to the great unknowable.

{ Guard them with all you've got. }

"My poetry was never written for a nation in crisis, obviously, if you've read any. But my poems and lots of people's poems are unintentional responses to terrorism, in that they honor life."

—Billy Collins, poet,
interviewed in *Mother Jones*

Yes, it's an awful world. When we write, we fling ourselves into the abyss in the hope of returning with something worthy, lasting, even beautiful.

{ This is no small thing we do. }

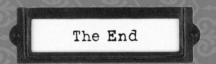

The End